Best Boba Brews

Surprise your Senses with 40 Boba
Bubble Tea Recipes to make at Home

BY

Daniel Humphreys

Copyright 2019 Daniel Humphreys

License Notes

Table of Contents

Introduction

Boba milk tea, pearl milk tea or bubble tea is a tea-based beverage created in the 1980's in the tea shops of Taichung in Taiwan.

However, what was once only a young girl's daily street drink in China, is gaining in popularity throughout the world.

The drink generally contains milk, fruit flavoring, and a tea base. Today though, boba bubble tea sellers often add taro, matcha powder or fresh fruit.

Bubble or boba tea is the perfect drink to enjoy any time of the day, and what's more, it is so easy to make at home. In fact, with a good selection of boba bubble tea recipes, you can experiment with lots of different flavors and teas until you discover your perfect blend.

All you need are the ingredients, starting with tapioca pearls which come in black, white or red. You can find these in specialized Asian food stores or online.

For a true boba bubble tea experience, you will also need a fat boba straw!

So, stock up on pearls and straws and get brewing with 40 Boba Bubble Tea Recipes to make at home.

How to Prepare the Boba Tapioca Pearls

Most bubble tea recipes state to prepare the tapioca pearls according to the package instructions. However, if you wish to prepare uncooked, dried large tapioca pearls you can follow this simple recipe. You can find boba online or at almost any Asian grocery store.

Servings: 1 (21 ounce) glass

Total Time: 1hour

Ingredients:

- 4-5 cups water
- 1 cup dried, large tapioca pearls
- ⅓ cup maple syrup

Directions:

1. On moderate to high heat, in a pan, bring the water to boil.

2. Add the tapioca pearls, stirring to prevent them from sticking.

3. As soon as the boba begin to float to the surface, reduce the heat to low-moderate and simmer for 20-25 minutes, stirring every 5-10 minutes.

4. Turn the heat off and allow the boba to rest it the water for between 10-15 minutes.

5. Drain and rinse in cold running water.

6. Add the prepared boba to a jar or bowl.

7. Cover with maple syrup and set to one side to rest before serving, for 15 minutes.

8. Best used within 2-3 hours of preparing.

Cook's Note: Never mix pearls with cold water.

Blackberry and Bourbon Boba Bubble Mint Tea

Bubble tea with a splash of bourbon is definitely for adults only!

Servings: 1

Total Time: 15mins

Ingredients:

- ½ cups dried, large pearl tapioca
- 2 ounces bourbon
- 2 tbsp maple syrup
- 1 cup strong brewed mint tea
- Angostura bitters
- Fresh mint

Directions:

1. Fill a small saucepan with cold water and bring to boil.

2. Add the tapioca and cook for 5 minutes.

3. Remove the tapioca, strain, and rinse with cold water.

4. Add the cooked tapioca to a tall glass.

5. Fill the glass will ice cubes.

6. Add the bourbon, followed by the maple syrup, mint tea, and 2 dashes of bitters.

7. Stir well. Garnish with mint. Serve with a fat straw and enjoy.

Blueberry Jam Bubble Tea

Combine chewy boba with sweet blueberry jam tea for an any time of the day drink.

Servings: 1

Total Time: 35mins

Ingredients:

- 3 tbsp tapioca pearls
- 4 tsp blueberry jam flavor tea
- ½ cup hot water
- 1-2 tbsp agave syrup
- 1 cup milk
- Ice

Directions:

1. First, cook the tapioca according to the package instructions.

2. Add the tea to hot water and brew for between 7-10 minutes.

3. Strain the tea into a bowl and transfer to the fridge to chill for a minimum of 10 minutes.

4. In a large glass, combine the tapioca pearls, agave syrup, and milk, stirring to combine.

5. Add ice along with the brewed tea and enjoy.

Bubble Tea Strawberry Margarita Cocktail

Boba tea with tequila-infused bubbles has to be the best and most fun cocktail ever!

Servings: 1-2

Total Time: 1hour

Ingredients:

- 1½ tbsp boba tapioca pearls
- 2 ounces silver tequila (divided)
- 2 Green tea bags
- 8 strawberries (hulled, sliced)
- 2 ounces strawberry margarita mix
- 1 ounce guava nectar
- 1 ounce heavy cream
- 6 ice cubes
- 1 tbsp sea salt
- Freshly squeezed juice of ½ lime
- 1 lime wedge (to garnish)

Directions:

1. First prepare the tapioca according to the packet instructions, straining off any excess water and transferring to a bowl. Add 1 ounce of silver tequila and put to one side.

2. Add each of the tea bags to ½ cup of hot water and steep for between 7-10 minutes. Remove and discard the tea bags before transferring to the fridge, to chill.

3. Add the strawberries, remaining tequila, margarita mix, guava nectar, fresh lime juice, cream, tea and ice cubes to a food blender and on the pulse setting, process until silky smooth.

4. Rim a martini glass with sea salt.

5. Add the tequila-infused pearls to the bottom of the glass(es).

6. Pour the margarita mixture over the pearls, garnish with a fresh lime wedge and serve.

Chamomile, Guava, and Rose Bubble Tea

Calming chamomile tea combines with fragrant rosebuds, sweet guava juice, and boba to deliver a soothing and calming drink.

Servings: 2

Total Time: 25mins

Ingredients:

- 2 cups water
- 1 chamomile tea bag
- 1 tsp culinary dried rose buds
- ¼ cup guava juice
- ¼ cup prepared boba tapioca pearls

Directions:

1. Boil the water and pour into to a jug, add the tea bag and rosebuds. Allow to steep for 3-5 minutes, before transferring to the fridge for 12-15 minutes, to cool.

2. Take the jug out of the refrigerator, discard the tea bag, and evenly divide the tea into 2 large glasses.

3. Add the guava juice to the tea and stir to combine.

4. Spoon the prepared boba into the glasses and serve.

Coco-Banana Boba

Super thick and indulgently creamy, this scrummy boba tastes like banana pudding in a glass.

Servings: 2

Total Time: 20mins

Ingredients:

- 6 cups water
- ⅓ cup boba tapioca pearls
- 8-9 drops liquid sweetener
- 2 tbsp canned coconut cream
- 1 medium banana (peeled, chopped, frozen)
- 1 (15 ounce) can coconut milk

Directions:

1. Bring the water to a boil in a saucepan and add the boba, Cook for 3-4 minutes, at a boil, before covering with a lid, turn the heat down to moderate and simmering for another 5-6 minutes.

2. Drain and rinse the boba, sweeten with liquid sweetener and set to one side.

3. Add the coconut cream, frozen banana, and coconut milk to a blender. Blitz until smooth.

4. Divide the boba between glasses and pour over the banana mixture. Enjoy straight away.

Creamy Avocado Boba

Chewy boba give great texture to an indulgently thick and creamy avocado smoothie.

Servings: 1

Total Time: 1hour 15mins

Ingredients:

- ⅓ cup prepared boba tapioca pearls
- 3 tbsp simple sugar syrup
- ⅓ cup almond milk
- 1 medium avocado (peeled, stoned)
- 1 cup ice
- ⅓ cup sweetened condensed milk

Directions:

1. Drain and rinse the just-prepared tapioca. Stir in 3 tbsp sugar syrup and set aside for an hour to soak.

2. Add the almond milk, avocado, ice, and condensed milk to a blender and blitz until smooth.

3. Spoon the boba into a glass and pour over the avocado mixture. Enjoy straight away.

English Breakfast Boba Tea

Wake-up to a chilled glass of breakfast bubble tea and get the day off to a great start.

Servings: 2

Total Time: 40mins

Ingredients:

- 2 English breakfast tea bags
- 2 tbsp superfine sugar
- 1 cup boiling water
- ¼ cup tapioca
- 1 cup milk
- 1 cup ice

Directions:

1. Add the tea bags along with the sugar and boiling water to a heatproof jug, stirring to dissolve the sugar. Set to one side for 4-6 minutes to allow the flavors to infuse.

2. Remove and discard the tea bags and transfer to the fridge to cool.

3. In a pan over high heat, bring 1½ quarts of cold water to boil.

4. Add the tapioca and turn the heat down to moderate to low and cook while occasionally stirring for between 20-30 minutes, until the tapioca is nearly clear and just tender. Drain the tapioca and rinse under cold running water. Transfer the mixture to a pitcher.

5. Add the tea mixture along with the milk to the tapioca, stirring gently to incorporate.

6. Divide the ice cubes between the chilled glasses and top with the tapioca mixture.

7. Enjoy.

Frozen Choc 'n Orange Bubble Tea

If you like frozen drinks and bubble tea, why not combine the two and blend this chocolate and orange tasty treat?

Servings: 2

Total Time: 45mins

Ingredients:

Orange syrup:

- ½ cup water
- ½ cup pure cane sugar
- Zest of 1 fresh orange
- Freshly squeezed juice of ½ orange

Bubble tea pearls:

- ½ cup quick-cook black tapioca pearls
- 4 cups water

Chocolate tea:

- 2 herbal orange tea bags
- 1½ cups hot water
- 2 tbsp cocoa powder
- 4-6 cups ice

Directions:

1. For the syrup, bring the water to boil. Take off the heat and stir in the sugar followed by the orange zest and fresh orange juice, stirring until the sugar entirely dissolves. Set to one side.

2. For the pearls, in a pan bring water to boil. Add the pearls, while gently stirring. Turn the heat down to low, and simmer while covered, cooking for 5 minutes.

3. Once the pearls are cooked, remove from the pan with a slotted spoon and add to the syrup, allowing the pearls to infuse for half an hour.

4. For the tea, add the orange tea bags to hot water and steep for between 4-6 minutes.

5. Remove and discard the tea bags.

6. Transfer the tea to a food blender. Add the cocoa powder to the tea and blend to combine.

7. Remove the jug from the blender and transfer to the fridge for half an hour.

8. Using a slotted spoon, remove the boba and divide between 2 large glasses.

9. Add the orange syrup to the blender, top with ice cubes and process until smooth and frothy.

10. Pour the frozen tea over the pearls and enjoy.

Ginger and Cardamom Bubble Tea

A spicy, zingy tea which is guaranteed to soothe and calm.

Servings: 1

Total Time: 1hour 30mins

Ingredients:

- ¼ cup prepared boba tapioca pearls
- 2-3 tbsp maple syrup
- ½" cube fresh ginger (peeled, sliced)
- 1⅔ cup water
- 1 cinnamon stick
- 2 green cardamom pods (split)
- 2 black tea bags
- ¾ cup + 1 tbsp almond milk

Directions:

1. Drain and rinse the just-prepared tapioca. Stir in maple syrup and set aside for an hour to soak.

2. Add the ginger, water, cinnamon, cardamom to a saucepan over moderately high heat and bring to a near boil.

3. Take off the heat and drop in the tea bags. Set aside for several minutes before straining the liquid into a jug, Set aside to cool. Discard any solids.

4. Spoon the boba into a glass. Pour over the tea mixture and top with almond milk. Enjoy straight away.

Green Apple Boba

A sweet and fruity treat with all the flavor of a crisp green apple.

Servings: 1

Total Time: 20mins

Ingredients:

- 2 cups water
- ½ cup boba tapioca pearls
- 1 cup ice
- ½ cup green apple flavored syrup
- 2 cups almond whole milk

Directions:

1. Bring the water to a boil in a saucepan and add the boba. Cook for approximately 25 minutes, until tender and chewy. Drain, rinse and set to one side to completely cool.

2. Add the ice, apple syrup, and milk to a blender, blitz until smooth.

3. Spoon the prepared boba into two glasses and pour over the apple mixture.

4. Serve straight away.

Green Boba Bubble Tea

This sweet and creamy boba tea is naturally green thanks to refreshing green tea and avocado. Yum!

Servings: 2

Total Time: 25mns

Ingredients:

- ¼ cup boba pearl tapioca
- 1 cup avocado (peeled, pitted, mashed)
- 1 cup green tea
- 6 ice cubes
- ½ cups sweetened condensed milk

Directions:

1. Prepare the tapioca according to the package instructions and set to one side.

2. Add the avocado, green tea, ice, and milk to a food blender and process.

3. Add the tapioca to a chilled glass.

4. Pour the avocado tea mixture over the tapioca.

5. Serve with a fat straw and enjoy.

Honeydew Bubble Tea

This popular boba tea flavor is a cross between a fruit dessert and a refreshing beverage.

Servings: 4

Total Time: 25mins

Ingredients:

- 10 cups water
- 1 cup of black tapioca pearls
- Agave syrup (to taste)
- 2 cups water
- ½ honeydew melon (rind removed, seeded, chopped into bite-size pieces)
- 1 cup soy milk
- 2 green tea bags

Directions:

1. In a large pan, bring the water to boil.

2. Add the tapioca and boil for 5 minutes until plump.

3. Cover the pan and reduce the heat to moderate, simmering for 5 minutes. Drain and set to one side.

4. Meanwhile, bring 2 cups of water to boil and steep the green tea bags. Transfer to the fridge to cool.

5. Add the melon to a food blender, and on pulse, process until smooth and transfer to the fridge.

6. As soon as the tea and melon puree are cooled, add both to a pitcher or jug.

7. Pour in the milk, taste and sweeten to taste.

8. When you are ready to serve, add 2-3 tbsp of tapioca pearls to a tall glass and fill with honeydew melon tea.

9. Serve and enjoy with a fat straw.

Honeyed Peach Boba Tea

Honey and peach are two foods that belong together, and this bubble tea is fruity, sweet and refreshing. In fact, it ticks all the flavor boxes.

Servings: 1-2

Total Time: 40mins

Ingredients:

- ½ cup boba pearl tapioca
- 2 tbsp + 1 tbsp honey (divided)
- 1 large, ripe peach (pitted, quartered)
- ½ cup black tea (chilled)
- ½ cup whole milk
- 6 ice cubes

Directions:

1. First, cook the boba according to the package directions. Drain, rinse and transfer to a bowl and stir in 2 tbsp of honey.

2. In a blender combine the peaches with the tea, whole milk, ice and 1 tbsp of honey. Stir.

3. Add a ¼ cup of honey-coated pearls to a glass.

4. Pour the tea over the pearls and serve with a fat straw.

5. Enjoy.

Lavender-Infused Earl Grey Boba Tea

If you like bubble tea, then you will love this recipe. Earl Grey tea is one of the most popular options for this creamy beverage and infusing the tea with lavender really takes it to new heights.

Servings: 2-3

Total Time: 35mins

Ingredients:

- 1 cup boba tapioca pearls
- Runny honey (to taste, divided)
- 1 tbsp culinary dried lavender flowers
- 3 cups boiling water
- 5 Earl Grey tea bags
- 1 tbsp sweetened condensed milk
- 2 cups whole milk

Directions:

1. Prepare the tapioca according to the pack instructions and mix with 1-2 spoonfuls of honey. Set aside until ready to use.

2. Make the tea by adding the lavender into a tea infuser and drop it into the boiling water along with the tea bags. Steep for several minutes.

3. Once brewed, remove, and discard the tea bags and lavender. Chill until ready to use.

4. To prepare the tea, add the cooked pearls to a glass, top with a spoonful of honey and condensed milk, stirring until combined.

5. Fill each glass ⅔ to the top with the tea.

6. Pour in the whole milk. Taste, and add additional honey or condensed milk.

Lychee Boba Tea

Once you discover the fruity and sweet flavors of this bubble milk tea, you won't be able to resist.

Servings: 1

Total Time: 20mins

Ingredients:

- ½ cup water
- 1 rooibos tea bag
- ½ cup canned lychee fruit in light syrup (drained)
- ½ cup almond milk
- 3 tbsp tapioca pearls (prepared, strained from syrup)
- 1-2 tsp simple syrup (from the tapioca pearls)
- Ice

Directions:

1. Heat the water to a gentle simmer and add the rooibos tea bag. Allow to steep for several minutes; the time will depend on how strong you prefer your tea.

2. In the meantime, in a food blender, on high speed, process the lychee and almond milk, until silky.

3. Add the cooked pearls to a large, tall glass.

4. Pour the lychee-milk mixture over the top of the tapioca.

5. Remove the tea bag from the water and add the tea.

6. Taste and add a little of the syrup that the tapioca pearls are cooked in.

7. Enjoy.

Mango Jasmine Boba

Syrupy honey boba is served under sweet mango and floral jasmine tea for a tropical treat.

Servings: 2

Total Time: 35mins

Ingredients:

- 2 cups water
- ¼ cup dried boba tapioca pearls
- Honey
- 1 cup whole milk
- 2 cups frozen chopped mango
- 1 cup brewed jasmine tea (cooled)

Directions:

1. Bring the water to a boil in a saucepan and add the boba. Stir occasionally while cooking for 15 minutes at a boil. Take off the heat and set aside, covered, for 15 more minutes.

2. Drain then rinse then boba. Stir in enough honey to make a syrupy mixture. Chill until ready to use.

3. Divide the chilled boba between two glasses.

4. Add the milk, mango, and tea to a blender and blitz until combined. Slowly pour the mixture over the boba in the glasses and serve.

Maple Coffee Cold Brew Boba

For those of you who want to try boba, but don't love tea, this invigorating maple-sweetened cold brew is the perfect option.

Servings: 2

Total Time: 1hour

Ingredients:

- 2 cups water
- ¼ cup boba tapioca pearls
- ½ cup simple sugar syrup
- 1 tbsp maple syrup
- ¼ cup cold-brewed coffee
- ½ cup whole milk

Directions:

1. Bring the water to a boil in a saucepan and add the boba. Stir until the boba float to the surface. Turn the heat down a little and cook for just over 12 minutes.

2. Take off the heat and set aside for another 12 minutes before draining and rinsing them. Pour the sugar syrup over the boba and stir well. Set aside to completely cool.

3. Stir the maple syrup into the coffee.

4. Spoon the boba into two glasses and pour over the coffee. Top each glass with milk.

5. Enjoy straight away.

Matcha Green Tea Boba

Get in on the matcha green tea trend with this tasty chilled boba treat.

Servings: 2

Total Time: 20mins

Ingredients:

- 1½ tsp matcha green tea powder
- 2 tbsp boiling water
- 1 cup whole milk
- 2 tbsp organic honey
- ½ cup ice
- 2 scoops green tea ice cream
- ¼ cup cooked boba tapioca pearls in syrup

Directions:

1. Dissolve the tea powder in the boiling water and set to one side to cool.

2. Add the cooled tea mixture to a cocktail mixer along with the milk, honey, and ice. Shake for 30-40 seconds until well chilled.

3. Divide the boba between two glasses, top each with one scoop of ice cream and then pour over the tea mixture,

4. Enjoy straight away.

Melting Chocolate and Strawberry Boba

An indulgent boba drink with melted chocolate and real strawberries. Dessert in a glass!

Servings: 1

Total Time: 15mins

Ingredients:

- 1 cup fresh strawberries (hulled, chopped)
- 3 tsp granulated sugar
- ¼ cup semisweet choc chips
- 2 tsp water
- 1 cup whole milk
- ½ cup brewed tea (cooled)
- 1 tbsp simple sugar syrup
- Ice
- 4 tbsp prepared boba pearl tapioca

Directions:

1. Add the strawberries to a blender along with 1½ tsp sugar. Blitz until you achieve a smooth puree.

2. Add the remaining sugar and choc chips to a small bowl and melt in the microwave, remove often to stir until silky. Stir the water into the melted chocolate.

3. Pour the pureed strawberries, milk, tea, sugar syrup, and melted chocolate into a cocktail mixer along with a handful of ice. Shake for 30-40 seconds until chilled.

4. Add the prepared boba to the base of a glass and pour over the strawberry chocolate mixture.

Mexican Horchata Bubble Tea

East meets west for a spicy and sensational boba tea.

Servings: 4

Total Time: 8hours

Ingredients:

Horchata:

- 1 cup raw almonds
- ½ cup basmati white rice
- 1 (3") cinnamon stick
- 5 cups filtered water (divided)

Boba:

- 5½ cups water (divided)
- 1 cup boba pearls
- 1 cup raw sugar

Directions:

1. In a single layer, spread the almonds on a baking sheet and in an oven set at 350 degrees F, roast until fragrant, for between 5-10 minutes.

2. In a grinder, pulverize the white rice together with the stick of cinnamon until finely ground. Transfer to a large bowl.

3. Add the toasted almonds to the bowl and cover with 2 cups of the filtered water. Cover the bowl and transfer to the fridge, overnight.

4. The following day, pour the contents of the bowl into the jug of food blender along with 2 more cups of filtered water. Process on high speed for between 1-2 minutes, until entirely smooth.

5. Pour the mixture through a cheesecloth-lined fine mesh sieve. Allow the majority of the liquid to drain through before gathering up the edges and squeezing out any remaining pulp. This will help to expel as much liquid as possible.

6. Transfer any leftover pulp to the blender along with 1 additional cup of filtered water and on high speed, blend for 1-2 minutes, before straining through the cheesecloth once more.

7. Transfer to the refrigerator until you are ready to serve. You will need to stir the mixture before serving.

8. To prepare the boba, bring 5 cups of the water the water to boil, and add the pearls, boiling for 5 minutes before

removing from the heat and setting to one side for 10 minutes.

9. While the boba cooks combine ½ cup of water and the raw sugar in a pan and boil for 1-2 minutes until the sugar entirely dissolves.

10. Remove the pan from the heat and transfer the mixture to a heat-safe bowl.

11. Using a slotted spoon, strain the boba and add to the sugar syrup. Set to one side to sit for 15 minutes.

12. To serve, evenly divided the boba between 4 glasses and add 2-3 teaspoonfuls of syrup.

13. Add the horchata and stir to incorporate, adding more sugar or syrup if needed, to sweeten.

Orange Blossom Honey Boba Tea

This bubble tea, sweetened with orange blossom honey and combined with calming chamomile tea is just perfect.

Servings: 1-2

Total Time: 20mins

Ingredients:

- 5 cups of water + ½ cup of water
- 2 chamomile tea bags
- ½ cup instant tapioca pearls
- 2 tbsp orange blossom honey
- ½ cup of almond milk

Directions:

1. Add ½ cup of water to cup and microwave for 60 seconds.

2. Add the tea bags to the water and allow too steep for 3 minutes. Set to one side to cool.

3. In a pan, bring 5 cups of water to boil and add the tapioca pearls.

4. As soon as the pearls float, cook on moderate heat for a few minutes.

5. Cover the pan and on low, simmer for 2-3 minutes.

6. Add the cooked pearls to cold water for 30 seconds.

7. Remove the pearls from the water and transfer to a dry, clean bowl.

8. Evenly coat the pearls in the orange blossom honey.

9. Transfer the coated pearls to a cup and add the tea, to the halfway mark.

10. Pour in the milk to fill the cup and enjoy.

Passion Fruit Boba Tea

Sweet and tangy passion fruit is an ideal fruit to add to boba tea; try it we know you will like it!

Servings: 4

Total Time: 1hour

Ingredients:

- 10-12 cups water
- 1 cup tapioca pearls
- 1 cup natural cane sugar
- 6 black tea bags
- 4 ounces passion fruit concentrate
- Almond milk

Directions:

1. Bring a large pan with a minimum of 10 cups of water to boil.

2. Cook the tapioca pearls according to the package instructions.

3. In the meantime, bring 1 cup water along with the sugar to boil in a pan, continually stirring until the sugar entirely dissolves.

4. Pour half of the sugar syrup over the tapioca pearls. Chill until cool.

5. Steep the black tea bags in 4 cups of extremely hot water for 8-10 minutes, depending on how strong you like your tea.

6. Remove and discard the tea bags and transfer to the fridge to cool. If you want to speed the cooling process up, you may add a few ice cubes.

7. Just before you are ready to serve, stir in the passion fruit concentrate along with ¼ - ½ cup of the remaining sugar syrup into the tea.

8. Spoon the prepared boba into 4 glasses, fill to 75 percent capacity with the tea mixture, and top with almond milk.

9. Serve and enjoy.

Peppermint Boba Tea

Experience a refreshing combination of chilled peppermint tea and sweet almond milk and enjoy a bubblicious tea.

Servings: 2

Total Time: 20mins

Ingredients:

- 1½ cups water
- 2 peppermint tea bags
- Tapioca pearls
- Ice cubes
- 1-2 cups sweetened almond milk
- Sprig of fresh mint (to garnish)

Directions:

1. Boil the water and steep the peppermint tea bags for 5 minutes, in a Mason jar.

2. Remove and discard the peppermint tea bags. Transfer the jar to the refrigerator to cool.

3. Prepare the tapioca pearls according to the package directions.

4. As soon as the pearls are cooked, add 2-3 spoonfuls to each of the 2 glasses.

5. Add a few ice cubes to each glass.

6. Evenly divide the tea between the glasses, and top with milk.

7. Garnish with mint and serve.

Pina Colada Bubble Tea

A true taste of the Caribbean in this tropical boba tea.

Servings: 1

Total Time: 7mins

Ingredients:

- ¼ cup fresh pineapple juice
- ½ cup coconut milk
- ¼ cup low-fat milk
- ¼ cup green or Earl Grey tea (brewed)
- 1 tbsp sugar syrup
- 2-4 tbsp prepared tapioca pearls
- Ice

Directions:

1. Add the pineapple juice, coconut milk, low-fat milk, brewed tea and sugar syrup to a cocktail shaker and shake it all about until bubbles begin to form on the surface, and the mixture is frothy, this will take around 10-15 seconds.

2. Add the prepared tapioca pearls to a large, tall glass.

3. Pour the pineapple mixture over the pearls, add ice and enjoy with a fat straw.

Pineapple Bubble Tea Smoothie

A thick and creamy tropical pineapple smoothie sits on top of chewy boba for a tasty afternoon treat.

Servings: 2

Total Time: 30mins

Ingredients:

Boba syrup:

- ½ cup water
- ¼ cup brown sugar
- ¼ cup granulated sugar

Smoothie:

- 3½ cups water
- ¼ cup boba tapioca pearls
- ¾ cup Greek yogurt
- 2 cups fresh pineapple (chopped)
- 1 cup ice
- ¼ cup whole milk
- 2 ounces simple sugar syrup

Directions:

1. First, make the boba syrup. Add the water and sugars to a saucepan and bring to a boil. Continue to stir and heat until the sugar dissolves. Take off the heat and allow to completely cool.

2. Next, prepare the boba. Bring 3½ cups of water to a boil in a saucepan and add the boba. When the pearls pop up to the surface, cover with a lid and cook at a simmer for 5 minutes. Drain the boba and rinse well. Allow to cool. Pour over enough prepared sugar syrup to submerge the boba.

3. To make the smoothie, add the yogurt, pineapple, ice, milk, and 2 ounces sugar syrup to a blender and blitz until smooth.

4. Divide the pearls between two glasses and pour over the smoothie. Enjoy straight away.

Pistachio Boba Tea

Add a little texture with pistachio pudding mix to this creamy, nutty bubble tea.

Servings: 6

Total Time: 5mins

Ingredients:

- ½ cup evaporated milk
- ½ cup whole milk
- ½ cup green or white tea (brewed)
- 2 tbsp pistachio pudding mix
- 1 tbsp sugar syrup
- Green food coloring (optional)
- 2-4 tbsp tapioca (cooked)

Directions:

1. Add the milks, tea, pudding mix, sugar syrup, green food coloring (optional) and ice to a cocktail shaker and shake it all about for 10-15 seconds.

2. Add the tapioca pearls to the bottom of a tall glass.

3. Pour the tea over the tapioca.

4. Add ice and enjoy.

Pretty Pink Bubble Tea with Cherry and Hibiscus

A pretty pink fruity bubble tea which is a pleasure to the eyes and the taste buds.

Servings: 2

Total Time: 1hour 20mins

Ingredients:

- 2 hibiscus tea bags
- 1 cup boiling water
- 2 cups water
- ¼ cup boba tapioca pearls
- ½ cup water
- ½ cup granulated sugar
- 2 tbsp tart cherry juice
- Sweetened condensed milk
- Ice

Directions:

1. Steep the tea bags in the cup of boiling water for 15-20 minutes. Squeeze the tea bags then discard. Chill the tea until cold.

2. Add 2 cups of water to a saucepan over high heat and bring to a boil. Add the boba, turn the heat down a little and simmer for 3-4 minutes. Take off the heat, cover with a lid and set aside for 10-12 minutes.

3. In a second saucepan over moderate heat, add ½ a cup of water and the sugar. Heat, while stirring, until the sugar dissolves. Take off the heat and allow to cool.

4. Drain the tapioca and spoon equally into glasses.

5. Add the cherry juice, condensed milk, chilled tea, ice, and 2 tbsp of the prepared sugar syrup to a cocktail mixer and shake for 40-50 seconds. Strain the mixture into the glasses over the boba.

6. Enjoy straight away.

Pumpkin Spice Chai Bubble Tea

All the fragrant, spicy flavor of fresh pumpkin pie and chai tea in one glass. What's more, you'll have a little homemade pumpkin pie creamer left over to spice up other recipes, or even your morning coffee.

Servings: 2

Total Time: 30mins

Ingredients:

Pumpkin Pie Creamer:

- 1½ tbsp pureed pumpkin
- ⅔ cup almond milk
- 2 tbsp coconut sugar
- ¾ tsp pumpkin pie spice flavoring

Bubble Tea:

- Water
- ¼ cup boba tapioca pearls
- 1 tbsp coconut sugar
- 12 ounces strong brewed chai tea (chilled)

Directions:

1. First, make the creamer. Whisk together the pureed pumpkin, milk, sugar, and pumpkin pie flavoring. Chill until ready to use.

2. Next, prepare the boba. Pour 7-8" of water into a saucepan and bring to a boil. Add the boba and simmer for several minutes, until tender. Take off the heat and drain away all but a ¼ cup of water from the pan. Stir in the coconut sugar and set to one side.

3. Spoon the boba into two glasses, pour over the chilled chai tea and top with the prepared pumpkin creamer.

4. Enjoy straight away.

Purple Taro Boba

Taro root gives this traditional boba a natural purple color.

Servings: 1

Total Time: 1hour 25mins

Ingredients:

- ⅓ cup prepared boba tapioca pearls
- 3 tbsp simple sugar syrup
- 1 small taro (peeled, cut into 1" cubes)
- Pinch baking soda
- ½ cup ice
- ¼ cup sweetened condensed milk
- ½ cup coconut milk

Directions:

1. Drain and rinse the just-prepared tapioca. Stir in 3 tbsp sugar syrup and set aside for an hour to soak.

2. Drain the taro and allow to completely cool. When cool, take one cube for the bubble tea and set the rest aside for another use.

3. Add the ice and both milks to a blender along with the cooled taro cube. Blitz until smooth.

4. Spoon the boba into the base of a glass and pour over the taro mixture Enjoy straight away.

Raspberry-Lime Green Boba Bubble Tea

Run out of tapioca pearls, no problem! You can substitute raspberry flavor gelatin for pearls.

Servings: 8

Total Time: 2hours 20mins

Ingredients:

- 12 cups water
- 16 matcha tea bags
- 4 tsp runny honey
- Freshly squeezed juice of 4 limes
- 1 (3 ounce) sachet raspberry gelatin

Directions:

1. First, brew the tea by heating the water. Add the matcha tea bags and allow to steep for 3-4 minutes before removing and discarding the tea bags.

2. Add the honey and stir to combine before transferring to the fridge for 60 minutes, to chill.

3. As soon as the tea is sufficiently cooled, add the lime juice.

4. Next, make the bubbles by mixing the raspberry gelatin according to the sachet directions. Transfer to the fridge for 60 minutes; remember to occasionally stir, to ensure that the gelatin is thickened rather than solid.

5. Add ice water to large mixing bowl and with a straw, trap a little of the prepared gelatin in the straw, allowing it to drip slowly into the bowl. When the gelatin hits the water, orbs should begin to form and sink to the bottom of the mixing bowl.

6. Take the ice out of the bowl and pour the mixture into a mesh strainer.

7. Transfer the orbs from the mesh strainer into a bowl and refrigerate.

8. To prepare the tea, pour the tea mixture over ice, add 2-3 spoonfuls of orbs and serve with a fat straw.

Raspberry Mascarpone Boba

A sophisticated boba bubble treat with fresh mascarpone, raspberry juice, and honey,

Servings: 4-6

Total Time: 30mins

Ingredients:

- 4 cups water
- ½ cup boba tapioca pearls
- 2 tbsp organic honey
- ⅓ cup fresh mascarpone
- 2 cups raspberry juice
- 1½ cups brewed black tea (cold)
- 1 cup whole milk

Directions:

1. Bring the water to a boil in a saucepan and add the boba, Cook for 3-4 minutes, at a boil, before covering with a lid, turn the heat down to moderate and simmering for another 5-6 minutes.

2. Drain and rinse the boba, set to one side.

3. Whisk together the honey and mascarpone. When combined, whisk in the raspberry juice, tea, and milk. Chill until cold.

4. Divide the boba between glasses and top with chilled raspberry/mascarpone mixture.

Red Bean Bubble Tea

Red bean paste is widely used in Asian cuisines, dessert specifically, and can be easily found in your nearest ethnic grocery store.

Servings: 2

Total Time: 30mins

Ingredients:

- 2 tbsp brown sugar
- 2 tbsp water
- 6 cups water
- ⅓ cup boba tapioca pearls
- 3 cups whole milk
- ⅔ cup sweet red bean paste

Directions:

1. Add 2 tbsp brown sugar and 2 tbsp water to a small bowl and heat in the microwave until the sugar dissolves. Stir well.

2. Bring the 6 cups of water to a boil in a saucepan and add the boba, cook for 3-4 minutes, covered with a lid at a simmer, before uncovering and cooking for another 3-4 minutes.

3. Drain the boba, rinse it and stir in the prepared brown sugar syrup. Allow to cool.

4. Add the milk and red bean paste to a blender, pulsing until combined.

5. Divide the cool boba pearls between glasses and pour over the red bean mixture.

Tangy Tangerine Boba Tea

Your teens will love this bubble tea. It's tangy, sweet and creamy.

Servings: 2

Total Time: 35mins

Ingredients:

- 2 tbsp tapioca pearls (prepared)
- 1 cup green tea
- Freshly squeezed juice of 3 tangerines (1 cup)
- 2 tbsp runny honey
- ½ cup coconut milk

Directions:

1. Prepare the tapioca pearls as directed on the package, this will take around 20 minutes.

2. Make one cup of green tea, to your preferred strength and allow to cool to room temperature.

3. Using a whisk, combine the cooled green tea, with the fresh tangerine juice and honey for 60 seconds, until combined.

4. Evenly divide the mixture between 2, tall glasses.

5. Transfer 1 tablespoon of prepared tapioca pearls to each glass.

6. Add the desired amount of milk to each glass and stir; the amount of milk will depend on how milky you like your tea.

7. Serve with a fat straw and enjoy.

Thai Boba with Sweet Almond Syrup

Boba tea is originally Taiwanese, but this delicious recipe is inspired by Thai flavors for a true taste of Asia.

Servings: 2

Total Time: 40mins

Ingredients:

- 5 cups water
- ½ cup boba tapioca pearls
- ½ cup brown sugar
- ½ cup water
- ¼ cup almond flavored syrup
- 3 black tea bags
- 2 cups boiling hot water
- ½ cup almond milk

Directions:

1. Bring the 5 cups of water to a boil in a saucepan and add the boba, cook for 5 minutes, at a boil, before taking off the heat and setting aside for 10-12 minutes.

2. In the meantime, add the brown sugar and ½ cup water to a second saucepan and bring to boil, while stirring, until the sugar dissolves. Take off the heat and transfer to a bowl.

3. Add the almond syrup to the prepared sugar syrup and stir to combine.

4. Drain the boba, rinse with water and add to the syrup mixture. Stir and set aside for 10-12 minutes.

5. Steep the tea bags in hot water for several minutes. Squeeze the bags before discarding and chill the tea until cold.

6. Spoon the soaked boba into two glasses, divide the tea between the glasses and top with almond milk.

7. Enjoy straight away.

Traditional Milky Bubble Tea

Forget the fancy flavors and exotic fruits, sometimes original is best and this milky black tea boba ticks all the boxes.

Servings: 1

Total Time: 20mins

Ingredients:

- ⅓ cup prepared boba tapioca pearls
- 4 tbsp simple sugar syrup
- ½ cup strong-brewed black tea (cool)
- ⅔ cup ice
- ½ cup whole milk (chilled)

Directions:

5. Drain and rinse the just-prepared tapioca. Stir in 3 tbsp sugar syrup and set aside for an hour to soak.

6. Add the cool tea, 1 tbsp sugar syrup, and ice to a cocktail mixer and shake for 30-40 seconds until chilled.

7. Spoon the boba into the bottom of a glass, pour over the chilled tea and top with milk.

8. Enjoy straight away.

Vanilla Bean Lychee-Coconut Cooler with

A truly tropical affair with sweet coconut, exotic lychee, and aromatic vanilla beans.

Servings: 2

Total Time: 2hours

Ingredients:

- 4 cups water
- ½ cup boba tapioca pearls
- 2 cups coconut milk
- 10 fresh lychees (peeled)
- Scrapings of a 1" piece of vanilla bean
- Pinch salt
- 1¼ cups almond milk

Directions:

1. Bring the water to a boil in a saucepan and add the boba, cook for 3-4 minutes, at a boil, before covering with a lid, turn the heat down to moderate and simmering for another 5-6 minutes.

2. Drain and rinse the boba, transfer to a container, cover with fresh water and chill until ready to serve.

3. Add the coconut milk, lychees, vanilla bean scrapings, salt, and almond milk to a blender and blitz until smooth. Chill the coconut milk mixture for half an hour before transferring to the freezer for an hour.

4. Spoon the cooled boba into two glasses and pour over the chilled coconut milk mixture. Serve straight away.

Vanilla Chai Irish Cream Spiked Boba Tea

A truly grown-up bubble tea spiked with Irish Cream is the perfect pick-me-up.

Servings: 1-2

Total Time: 1hour 15mins

Ingredients:

- 1 cup sugar
- 5 cups of water (divided)
- 1 vanilla bean
- 2 tsp vanilla essence
- ¼ cup dried tapioca pearls
- 2 chai tea bags
- ⅓ cup Irish Cream

To serve:

- Whipped cream
- Chocolate shavings
- Cinnamon sticks

Directions:

1. First, make the vanilla syrup by combining the sugar and 1 cup of water in a pan. Cut the vanilla bean open, and carefully scrape the seeds into the pan along with the pod itself and the vanilla essence. Over moderate to high heat, bring to boil and on low, simmer for 15 minutes. Remove the pod and put to one side to cool.

2. Next, prepare the boba by filling a small pan with 2 cups of water and boil. Add the tapioca pearls, stirring to combine. Set the heat to moderate and cook for between 5-10 minutes. Remove the pan from the heat, cover and set to one side for 20 minutes.

3. Drain the boba and soak it in the vanilla syrup until you are ready to prepare the tea.

4. Take 2 cups of boiling water, add a tea bag to each and allow the tea to steep for 12-15 minutes. After which, remove and discard the tea bags. Set the tea to one side to cool before transferring to the fridge to chill.

5. Add the boba to 2 glasses, pour over the syrup and add ice.

6. Pour the now chilled tea over the ice and add the Irish Cream, while stirring to combine.

7. Garnish with cream, chocolate shavings and a stick of cinnamon.

8. Serve with a fat straw.

Watermelon Bubble Tea

So much more than just a beverage, this boba tea is a refreshing snack.

Servings: 4

Total Time: 45mins

Ingredients:

- 5 cups watermelon (peeled, seeded, chopped)
- 4 cups water
- 1 cup of dried tapioca pearls
- 5 cups black tea (lukewarm)
- ¼ cup condensed milk
- Ice

Directions:

1. In a blender chop the watermelon until smooth.

2. In a pan bring the water to boil and add the pearls, boil until the boba is soft inside and plumped up.

3. Remove the boba from the water and allow to cool in a drop of the cooking water as this will prevent the boba from sticking.

4. In a jug, combine the watermelon with the warm black tea and milk, stirring until the ingredients are fully combined.

5. Add ¼ cup of the boba to each of the 4 tall glasses, fill with ice, top with the tea and enjoy.

Zingy Kiwi Bubble Tea

Who doesn't love the sweet 'n sour flavor of fresh kiwifruit?! What's more, it's packed full of fiber, calcium, and vitamin C.

Servings: 3

Total Time: 20mins

Ingredients:

- 4 cups water
- ½ cup large tapioca pearls
- ½ cup skim milk
- ¼ cup sweetened condensed milk
- 1 cup ice
- 3 kiwifruit (peeled, sliced)

Directions:

1. Bring the water to a boil in a saucepan and add the tapioca. Boil for 3-4 minutes until soft. Drain and rinse. Allow to completely cool.

2. Divide the cooled pearls between 3 glasses.

3. Add the milks and ice to a blender and blitz until smooth. Add the kiwifruit and blitz again until just combined. Pour the mixture into the glasses and enjoy straight away,

Author's Afterthoughts

Thanks ever so much to each of my cherished readers for investing the time to read this book!

I know you could have picked from many other books but you chose this one. So a big thanks for downloading this book and reading all the way to the end.

If you enjoyed this book or received value from it, I'd like to ask you for a favor. Please take a few minutes to post an honest and heartfelt review on Amazon.com. Your support does make a difference and helps to benefit other people.

Thanks!

Daniel Humphreys

About the Author

Daniel Humphreys

Many people will ask me if I am German or Norman, and my answer is that I am 100% unique! Joking aside, I owe my cooking influence mainly to my mother who was British! I can certainly make a mean Sheppard's pie, but when it comes to preparing Bratwurst sausages and drinking beer with friends, I am also all in!

I am taking you on this culinary journey with me and hope you can appreciate my diversified background. In my 15 years career as a chef, I never had a dish returned to me by one of clients, so that should say something about me!

Actually, I will take that back. My worst critic is my four years old son, who refuses to taste anything that is green color. That shall pass, I am sure.

My hope is to help my children discover the joy of cooking and sharing their creations with their loved ones, like I did all my life. When you develop a passion for cooking and my suspicious is that you have one as well, it usually sticks for life. The best advice I can give anyone as a professional chef is invest. Invest your time, your heart in each meal you are creating. Invest also a little money in good cooking hardware and quality ingredients. But most of all enjoy every meal you prepare with YOUR friends and family!

Made in the USA
Monee, IL
09 November 2019